The Allo Gardener's Log Book

Name: _JOHN STRUTHERS_

Date: _____

Notes

HOZELOCK   ANTI TWIST

TRICOFLEX   "   KINK.

MANURE — ANDY — 07710 485171

Plant Name	Date Planted

Water Requirements 💧 💧💧 💧💧💧   Sunlight ☀ ☀ ⬤

☐ Seed   ☐ Transplant

Date	Event

Notes

Outcome

Uses

Purchased at: _____   Price: _____

Plant Name	Date Planted

Water Requirements 💧 💧💧 💧💧💧   Sunlight ☀ ☀ ⬤

☐ Seed   ☐ Transplant

Date	Event

Notes

Outcome

Uses

Purchased at: _____   Price: _____

Plant Name	Date Planted

Water Requirements 💧 💧💧 💧💧💧   Sunlight ☀ ☀ ●

☐ Seed   ☐ Transplant

Date	Event

Notes

Outcome

Uses

Purchased at: _____   Price: _____

Plant Name	Date Planted

Water
Requirements 💧 💧💧 💧💧💧   Sunlight ☀ ☀ ⬤

☐ Seed   ☐ Transplant

Date	Event

Notes

Outcome

Uses

Purchased at: _____   Price: _____

Plant Name	Date Planted

Water Requirements 💧 💧💧 💧💧💧　　Sunlight ☀ ◐ ●

☐ Seed　　☐ Transplant

Date	Event

Notes

Outcome

Uses

Purchased at: _____　　Price: _____

Plant Name	Date Planted

Water
Requirements 💧 💧💧 💧💧💧   Sunlight ☀ ☀ ⬤

☐ Seed   ☐ Transplant

Date	Event

Notes

Outcome

Uses

Purchased at: _____   Price: _____

Plant Name	Date Planted

Water Requirements 💧 💧💧 💧💧💧   Sunlight ☀ ☼ ●

☐ Seed   ☐ Transplant

Date	Event

Notes

Outcome

Uses

Purchased at: _____   Price: _____

Plant Name	Date Planted

Water
Requirements 💧　💧💧　💧💧💧　　　Sunlight ☀ ☀ ⚫

☐ Seed　　☐ Transplant

Date	Event

Notes

Outcome

Uses

Purchased at: _____　　Price: _____

Plant Name	Date Planted

Water Requirements 💧 💧💧 💧💧💧   **Sunlight** ☼ ◑ ●

☐ Seed   ☐ Transplant

Date	Event

Notes

Outcome

Uses

Purchased at: _____   Price: _____

Plant Name	Date Planted

Water Requirements 💧 💧💧 💧💧💧

Sunlight ☀ ☀ ⬤

☐ Seed ☐ Transplant

Date	Event

Notes

Outcome

Uses

Purchased at: _____ Price: _____

Plant Name	Date Planted

Water
Requirements 💧 💧💧 💧💧💧   Sunlight ☀ ◐ ●

☐ Seed   ☐ Transplant

Date	Event

Notes

Outcome

Uses

Purchased at: _____   Price: _____

Plant Name	Date Planted

Water
Requirements 💧 💧💧 💧💧💧   Sunlight ☀ ☀ ●

☐ Seed   ☐ Transplant

Date	Event

Notes

Outcome

Uses

Purchased at: _____   Price: _____

Plant Name	Date Planted

Water
Requirements 💧 💧💧 💧💧💧   Sunlight ☀ ☀ ⬤

☐ Seed   ☐ Transplant

Date	Event

Notes

Outcome

Uses

Purchased at: _____ Price: _____

Plant Name	Date Planted

Water
Requirements 💧 💧💧 💧💧💧   Sunlight ☀ ☀ ●

☐ Seed   ☐ Transplant

Date	Event

Notes

Outcome

Uses

Purchased at: _____   Price: _____

Plant Name	Date Planted

Water Requirements 💧 💧💧 💧💧💧   Sunlight ☀ ◐ ⬤

☐ Seed   ☐ Transplant

Date	Event

Notes

Outcome

Uses

Purchased at: _____   Price: _____

Plant Name | Date Planted

Water Requirements ● ●● ●●●   Sunlight ☀ ☽ ●

☐ Seed   ☐ Transplant

Date	Event

Notes

Outcome

Uses

Purchased at: _____   Price: _____

Plant Name	Date Planted

Water Requirements 💧 💧💧 💧💧💧   Sunlight ☀ ☀ ●

☐ Seed   ☐ Transplant

Date	Event

Notes

Outcome

Uses

Purchased at: _____   Price: _____

Plant Name	Date Planted

Water Requirements 💧 💧💧 💧💧💧   Sunlight ☀ ☀ ●

☐ Seed   ☐ Transplant

Date	Event

Notes

Outcome

Uses

Purchased at: _____   Price: _____

Plant Name	Date Planted

Water Requirements 🌢 🌢🌢 🌢🌢🌢   Sunlight ☀ ☀ ●

☐ Seed   ☐ Transplant

Date	Event

Notes

Outcome

Uses

Purchased at: _____ Price: _____

Plant Name	Date Planted

Water Requirements 💧 💧💧 💧💧💧   Sunlight ☀ 🌤 ⚫

☐ Seed   ☐ Transplant

Date	Event

Notes

Outcome

Uses

Purchased at: _____   Price: _____

Plant Name	Date Planted

Water Requirements 💧 💧💧 💧💧💧　　Sunlight ☼ ☼ ●

☐ Seed　　☐ Transplant

Date	Event

Notes

Outcome

Uses

Purchased at: _____ Price: _____

Plant Name	Date Planted

Water
Requirements ⬤ ⬤⬤ ⬤⬤⬤   Sunlight ☀ ☀ ⬤

☐ Seed   ☐ Transplant

Date	Event

Notes

Outcome

Uses

Purchased at: _____   Price: _____

Plant Name	Date Planted

Water Requirements 💧 💧💧 💧💧💧   Sunlight ☀ ☀ ●

☐ Seed   ☐ Transplant

Date	Event

Notes

Outcome

Uses

Purchased at: _____   Price: _____

Plant Name	Date Planted

Water
Requirements 💧 💧💧 💧💧💧   Sunlight ☀ 🌤 ⚫

☐ Seed   ☐ Transplant

Date	Event

Notes

Outcome

Uses

Purchased at: _____   Price: _____

Plant Name	Date Planted

Water
Requirements 💧 💧💧 💧💧💧   Sunlight ☀ ☀ ⚫

☐ Seed   ☐ Transplant

Date	Event

Notes

Outcome

Uses

Purchased at: _____   Price: _____

Plant Name	Date Planted

Water
Requirements 💧 💧💧 💧💧💧   Sunlight ☀ ☀ ⚫

☐ Seed   ☐ Transplant

Date	Event

Notes

Outcome

Uses

Purchased at: _____   Price: _____

Plant Name	Date Planted

Water Requirements 💧 💧💧 💧💧💧   Sunlight ☼ ☼ ⬤

☐ Seed   ☐ Transplant

Date	Event

Notes

Outcome

Uses

Purchased at: _____   Price: _____

Plant Name	Date Planted

Water
Requirements 💧 💧💧 💧💧💧   Sunlight ☀ ◑ ⬤

☐ Seed   ☐ Transplant

Date	Event

Notes

Outcome

Uses

Purchased at: _____ Price: _____

Plant Name	Date Planted

Water
Requirements 💧 💧💧 💧💧💧   Sunlight ☀ ◑ ●

☐ Seed   ☐ Transplant

Date	Event

Notes

Outcome

Uses

Purchased at: _____   Price: _____

Plant Name	Date Planted

Water Requirements 💧 💧💧 💧💧💧   Sunlight ☀ ☀ ●

☐ Seed   ☐ Transplant

Date	Event

Notes

Outcome

Uses

Purchased at: _____   Price: _____

Plant Name	Date Planted

Water
Requirements 🌢 🌢🌢 🌢🌢🌢   Sunlight ☀ ☼ ●

☐ Seed   ☐ Transplant

Date	Event

Notes

Outcome

Uses

Purchased at: _____   Price: _____

Plant Name	Date Planted

Water Requirements 🌢 🌢🌢 🌢🌢🌢   Sunlight ☀ ☀ ●

☐ Seed   ☐ Transplant

Date	Event

Notes

Outcome

Uses

Purchased at: _____   Price: _____

Plant Name	Date Planted

Water Requirements 💧 💧💧 💧💧💧   Sunlight ☀ ☀ ⬤

☐ Seed   ☐ Transplant

Date	Event

Notes

Outcome

Uses

Purchased at: _____   Price: _____

Plant Name	Date Planted

Water Requirements 💧 💧💧 💧💧💧   Sunlight ☼ ☼ ●

☐ Seed   ☐ Transplant

Date	Event

Notes

Outcome

Uses

Purchased at: _____   Price: _____

Plant Name	Date Planted

Water
Requirements 💧 💧💧 💧💧💧   Sunlight ☀ ☽ ●

☐ Seed   ☐ Transplant

Date	Event

Notes

Outcome

Uses

Purchased at: _____   Price: _____

Plant Name	Date Planted

Water Requirements 💧 💧💧 💧💧💧   Sunlight ☀ ☀ ●

☐ Seed   ☐ Transplant

Date	Event

Notes

Outcome

Uses

Purchased at: _____   Price: _____

Plant Name	Date Planted

Water Requirements 💧 💧💧 💧💧💧   Sunlight ☀ ☀ ⬤

☐ Seed   ☐ Transplant

Date	Event

Notes

Outcome

Uses

Purchased at: _____   Price: _____

Plant Name	Date Planted

Water
Requirements 🌢 🌢🌢 🌢🌢🌢   Sunlight ☀ ☀ ●

☐ Seed   ☐ Transplant

Date	Event

Notes

Outcome

Uses

Purchased at: _____ Price: _____

Plant Name	Date Planted

Water Requirements 💧 💧💧 💧💧💧   Sunlight ☀ ☀ ⬤

☐ Seed   ☐ Transplant

Date	Event

Notes

Outcome

Uses

Purchased at: _____   Price: _____

Plant Name	Date Planted

Water
Requirements 💧　💧💧　💧💧💧　　Sunlight ☀ ☀ ⬤

☐ Seed　　☐ Transplant

Date	Event

Notes

Outcome

Uses

Purchased at: _____　Price: _____

Plant Name	Date Planted

Water
Requirements 💧 💧💧 💧💧💧   Sunlight ☀ ☀ ⚫

☐ Seed   ☐ Transplant

Date	Event

Notes

Outcome

Uses

Purchased at: _____   Price: _____

Plant Name	Date Planted

Water Requirements 💧 💧💧 💧💧💧   Sunlight ☀ ☽

☐ Seed   ☐ Transplant

Date	Event

Notes

Outcome

Uses

Purchased at: _____   Price: _____

Plant Name	Date Planted

Water Requirements 💧 💧💧 💧💧💧   Sunlight ☀ ◑ ●

☐ Seed   ☐ Transplant

Date	Event

Notes

Outcome

Uses

Purchased at: _____   Price: _____

Plant Name	Date Planted

Water Requirements 💧 💧💧 💧💧💧   Sunlight ☀ 🌤 ⚫

☐ Seed   ☐ Transplant

Date	Event

Notes

Outcome

Uses

Purchased at: _____   Price: _____

Plant Name	Date Planted

Water Requirements 💧 💧💧 💧💧💧   Sunlight ☀ ☀ ⚫

☐ Seed   ☐ Transplant

Date	Event

Notes

Outcome

Uses

Purchased at: _____   Price: _____

Plant Name	Date Planted

Water Requirements 🌢 🌢🌢 🌢🌢🌢

Sunlight ☀ ☀ ●

☐ Seed   ☐ Transplant

Date	Event

Notes

Outcome

Uses

Purchased at: _____   Price: _____

Plant Name	Date Planted

Water
Requirements 💧 💧💧 💧💧💧   Sunlight ☀ ☽ ⬤

☐ Seed   ☐ Transplant

Date	Event

Notes

Outcome

Uses

Purchased at: _____   Price: _____

Plant Name	Date Planted

Water Requirements ◌ ◌◌ ◌◌◌

Sunlight ☀ ☀ ●

☐ Seed   ☐ Transplant

Date	Event

Notes

Outcome

Uses

Purchased at: _____ Price: _____

Plant Name	Date Planted

Water Requirements 💧 💧💧 💧💧💧   Sunlight ☀ ☀ ●

☐ Seed   ☐ Transplant

Date	Event

Notes

Outcome

Uses

Purchased at: _____   Price: _____

Plant Name	Date Planted

Water Requirements 💧 💧💧 💧💧💧   Sunlight ☀ ☀ ●

☐ Seed   ☐ Transplant

Date	Event

Notes

Outcome

Uses

Purchased at: _____   Price: _____

Plant Name	Date Planted

Water
Requirements 💧 💧💧 💧💧💧   Sunlight ☀ ☀ ●

☐ Seed   ☐ Transplant

Date	Event

Notes

Outcome

Uses

Purchased at: _____   Price: _____

Plant Name	Date Planted

Water
Requirements 💧 💧💧 💧💧💧   Sunlight ☼ ☼ ⬤

☐ Seed   ☐ Transplant

Date	Event

Notes

Outcome

Uses

Purchased at: _____   Price: _____

Plant Name	Date Planted

Water
Requirements 💧 💧💧 💧💧💧

Sunlight ☀ ◐ ●

☐ Seed   ☐ Transplant

Date	Event

Notes

Outcome

Uses

Purchased at: _____   Price: _____

Plant Name	Date Planted

Water Requirements 💧 💧💧 💧💧💧

Sunlight ☀ ◐ ●

☐ Seed   ☐ Transplant

Date	Event

Notes

Outcome

Uses

Purchased at: _____   Price: _____

Plant Name	Date Planted

Water
Requirements 💧 💧💧 💧💧💧   Sunlight ☼ ☼ ●

☐ Seed   ☐ Transplant

Date	Event

Notes

Outcome

Uses

Purchased at: _____ Price: _____

Plant Name	Date Planted

Water Requirements 🌢 🌢🌢 🌢🌢🌢   Sunlight ☼ ☽

☐ Seed   ☐ Transplant

Date	Event

Notes

Outcome

Uses

Purchased at: _____   Price: _____

Plant Name	Date Planted

Water Requirements 💧 💧💧 💧💧💧   Sunlight ☀ ☼ ●

☐ Seed   ☐ Transplant

Date	Event

Notes

Outcome

Uses

Purchased at: _____   Price: _____

Plant Name	Date Planted

Water Requirements 💧 💧💧 💧💧💧   Sunlight ☼ ☼ ●

☐ Seed   ☐ Transplant

Date	Event

Notes

Outcome

Uses

Purchased at: _____   Price: _____

Plant Name	Date Planted

Water Requirements 💧 💧💧 💧💧💧   Sunlight ☼ ◐ ●

☐ Seed   ☐ Transplant

Date	Event

Notes

Outcome

Uses

Purchased at: _____   Price: _____

Plant Name	Date Planted

Water Requirements 💧 💧💧 💧💧💧   Sunlight ☼ ☼ ●

☐ Seed   ☐ Transplant

Date	Event

Notes

Outcome

Uses

Purchased at: _____ Price: _____

Plant Name	Date Planted

Water Requirements 💧 💧💧 💧💧💧   Sunlight ☀ ☀ ●

☐ Seed   ☐ Transplant

Date	Event

Notes

Outcome

Uses

Purchased at: _____   Price: _____

Plant Name	Date Planted

Water Requirements 💧 💧💧 💧💧💧   Sunlight ☼ ☼ ●

☐ Seed   ☐ Transplant

Date	Event

Notes

Outcome

Uses

Purchased at: _____   Price: _____

Plant Name	Date Planted

Water Requirements 💧 💧💧 💧💧💧   Sunlight ☀ ◑ ●

☐ Seed   ☐ Transplant

Date	Event

Notes

Outcome

Uses

Purchased at: _____   Price: _____

Plant Name	Date Planted

Water Requirements 💧 💧💧 💧💧💧   Sunlight ☀ ☀ ⬤

☐ Seed   ☐ Transplant

Date	Event

Notes

Outcome

Uses

Purchased at: _____   Price: _____

Plant Name	Date Planted

Water Requirements 💧 💧💧 💧💧💧   Sunlight ☀ ☀ ⚫

☐ Seed   ☐ Transplant

Date	Event

Notes

Outcome

Uses

Purchased at: _____ Price: _____

Plant Name	Date Planted

Water Requirements 🌢 🌢🌢 🌢🌢🌢   Sunlight ☼ ☽ ●

☐ Seed   ☐ Transplant

Date	Event

Notes

Outcome

Uses

Purchased at: _____   Price: _____

Plant Name	Date Planted

Water Requirements 💧 💧💧 💧💧💧   Sunlight ☀ ☀ ⬤

☐ Seed   ☐ Transplant

Date	Event

Notes

Outcome

Uses

Purchased at: _____   Price: _____

Plant Name	Date Planted

Water Requirements 💧 💧💧 💧💧💧   Sunlight ☀ ☀ ●

☐ Seed   ☐ Transplant

Date	Event

Notes

Outcome

Uses

Purchased at: _____ Price: _____

Plant Name	Date Planted

Water Requirements 🌢 🌢🌢 🌢🌢🌢   Sunlight ☼ ☽ ●

☐ Seed   ☐ Transplant

Date	Event

Notes

Outcome

Uses

Purchased at: _____   Price: _____

Plant Name	Date Planted

Water Requirements 💧 💧💧 💧💧💧

Sunlight ☀ ☼ ●

☐ Seed ☐ Transplant

Date	Event

Notes

Outcome

Uses

Purchased at: _____ Price: _____

Plant Name	Date Planted

Water Requirements 💧 💧💧 💧💧💧   Sunlight ☀ ◐ ●

☐ Seed   ☐ Transplant

Date	Event

Notes

Outcome

Uses

Purchased at: _____   Price: _____

Plant Name		Date Planted

Water Requirements 💧 💧💧 💧💧💧   Sunlight ☀ - ◐ - ●

☐ Seed   ☐ Transplant

Date	Event

Notes

Outcome

Uses

Purchased at: _____   Price: _____

Plant Name	Date Planted

Water Requirements 💧 💧💧 💧💧💧   Sunlight ☀ ☀ ●

☐ Seed   ☐ Transplant

Date	Event

Notes

Outcome

Uses

Purchased at: _____   Price: _____

Plant Name	Date Planted

Water Requirements 💧 💧💧 💧💧💧   Sunlight ☀ ☀ ●

☐ Seed   ☐ Transplant

Date	Event

Notes

Outcome

Uses

Purchased at: _____   Price: _____

Plant Name	Date Planted

Water Requirements 💧 💧💧 💧💧💧   Sunlight ☀ ◐ ●

☐ Seed   ☐ Transplant

Date	Event

Notes

Outcome

Uses

Purchased at: _____   Price: _____

Plant Name	Date Planted

Water Requirements 💧 💧💧 💧💧💧

Sunlight ☀ ☀ ⬤

☐ Seed   ☐ Transplant

Date	Event

Notes

Outcome

Uses

Purchased at: _____ Price: _____

Plant Name   Date Planted

Water
Requirements 💧 💧💧 💧💧💧   Sunlight ☀ ◑ ⬤

☐ Seed   ☐ Transplant

Date	Event

Notes

Outcome

Uses

Purchased at: _____   Price: _____

Plant Name	Date Planted

Water Requirements 💧 💧💧 💧💧💧   Sunlight ☀ ◐ ⬤

☐ Seed   ☐ Transplant

Date	Event

Notes

Outcome

Uses

Purchased at: _____ Price: _____

Plant Name	Date Planted

Water Requirements 💧 💧💧 💧💧💧   Sunlight ☀ 🌤 ⚫

☐ Seed   ☐ Transplant

Date	Event

Notes

Outcome

Uses

Purchased at: _____   Price: _____

Plant Name	Date Planted

Water Requirements 💧 💧💧 💧💧💧   Sunlight ☼ ☼ ●

☐ Seed   ☐ Transplant

Date	Event

Notes

Outcome

Uses

Purchased at: _____   Price: _____

Plant Name	Date Planted

Water Requirements 💧 💧💧 💧💧💧   Sunlight ☀ ☽ ●

☐ Seed   ☐ Transplant

Date	Event

Notes

Outcome

Uses

Purchased at: _____   Price: _____

| Plant Name | Date Planted |

Water
Requirements 💧 💧💧 💧💧💧   Sunlight ☀ ☀ ⬤

☐ Seed   ☐ Transplant

Date	Event

Notes

Outcome

Uses

Purchased at: _____ Price: _____

Plant Name | Date Planted

Water Requirements 💧 💧💧 💧💧💧   Sunlight ☀ ☼ ●

☐ Seed   ☐ Transplant

Date	Event

Notes

Outcome

Uses

Purchased at: _____   Price: _____

Plant Name	Date Planted

Water Requirements 💧 💧💧 💧💧💧   Sunlight ☼ ☽ ●

☐ Seed   ☐ Transplant

Date	Event

Notes

Outcome

Uses

Purchased at: _____   Price: _____

Plant Name	Date Planted

Water Requirements 💧 💧💧 💧💧💧   Sunlight ☀ 🌤 ⬤

☐ Seed   ☐ Transplant

Date	Event

Notes

Outcome

Uses

Purchased at: _____   Price: _____

Plant Name		Date Planted

Water Requirements 💧 💧💧 💧💧💧   Sunlight ☼ ☼ ●

☐ Seed   ☐ Transplant

Date	Event

Notes

Outcome

Uses

Purchased at: _____   Price: _____

Plant Name	Date Planted

Water Requirements 💧 💧💧 💧💧💧   Sunlight ☀ ◐ ●

☐ Seed   ☐ Transplant

Date	Event

Notes

Outcome

Uses

Purchased at: _____   Price: _____

Plant Name	Date Planted

Water Requirements 💧 💧💧 💧💧💧   Sunlight ☀ ☼ ●

☐ Seed   ☐ Transplant

Date	Event

Notes

Outcome

Uses

Purchased at: _____   Price: _____

Plant Name	Date Planted

Water Requirements 💧 💧💧 💧💧💧   Sunlight ☀ ☀ ⬤

☐ Seed   ☐ Transplant

Date	Event

Notes

Outcome

Uses

Purchased at: _____   Price: _____

Plant Name	Date Planted

Water
Requirements 💧 💧💧 💧💧💧   Sunlight ☀ ☀

☐ Seed   ☐ Transplant

Date	Event

Notes

Outcome

Uses

Purchased at: _____   Price: _____

Printed in Great Britain
by Amazon